THE 100 BEST WAYS TO STAY TOGETHER

THE 100 BEST WAYS TO STAY TOGETHER

Simple Truths, Surprising Insights into What Makes Relationships Work, and What Makes Relationships Last

Ben White

A Dell Book

Published by
Dell Publishing
a division of
Bantam Doubleday Dell Publishing Group, Inc.
1540 Broadway
New York, New York 10036

ISBN: 0-440-22573-6

Printed in the United States of America

Published simultaneously in Canada

March 1998

10 9 8 7 6 5 4 3 2 1

OPM

Dedicated to every person who understands
that pain that's shared is cut in half,
and joy that's shared is doubled.

To *Donna Seager,* because to be touched by her is to truly understand what it is to find love, joy and wonder in people, the world, and life itself.

To *Esther Copeland,* my sister, whose heart encompasses her whole person and whose love knows no bounds.

To Esther and John, Joy and Norm, Eileen and Ken, Lynda and Darrel, Barbara and Ralph, Maryam and Bob, and the other couples I know and hold dear, whose relationships prove that the principles in my book really work.

Millions upon millions of us have been victimized almost from birth and all of our lives by a woman named Cinderella.

Is there anyone who doesn't remember the last sentence of the story? "And they lived happily ever after."

Did they? How? For instance, do you think it was all roses with Cinderella's mother-in-law? How did the queen feel about this little nobody her son found, when Mom had a princess all picked out in another kingdom? What about when the prince stayed out late jousting with the guys? Or when Cinderella had a headache? Or when the prince's hair started to thin, or when Cindy put on a little weight after the third little prince was born and . . .

Nope, the last words on the subject were "happily ever after." And *we bought it.*

Most of us have integrated this story and a lot of other stories like it into our worldview, and our expectations and hopes for ourselves. We've read or seen countless books and films that pretty much parallel the Cinderella story too. Bogart got Bacall, Harry got Sally, and thousands of similar fantasies are constantly zapping us and reinforcing the same essential programming—all in the face of some very contradictory realities.

Well, Cindy, you've come a long way, baby. I must know a dozen Cinderellas with nice homes, often with kids, and no prince anywhere in sight. Their princes came, all right, but then they left. So much for the happily-ever-after part.

Conversely, I know plenty of princes with tales of woe and misunderstanding, whose wives left them for other guys, second chances, and richer kingdoms.

And then there are the countless single men and women who simply can't make any relationship last more than a few years. (As you may know, the contemporary nomenclature for it is "serial monogamy.")

What's going on here? Where's the happy ending I thought was my birthright? Where's a reliable fairy-godmother when you really need one?

I recently dined with an attractive single mother and professional woman who made an observation that I've now heard from many people. After relating the story of a recent disastrous relationship, she sighed: "I'm beginning to wonder if marriage is an idea that works anymore." (From her lips to my mother's ears; miles away an icicle surely went through Mom's heart. At each family reunion she asks, "When's the wedding?")

And though this woman's comment was hardly new or profound, it got me thinking, reexamining assumptions made and accepted long ago.

Does marriage work, at least as so many of us have come to expect it? I wondered. I tried to think of happily married couples I knew, realizing that with only a few exceptions, I couldn't say for certain whether most are truly, deeply, permanently, happily married or not.

I considered that for well over a decade my own marriage was one that was openly envied by friends as one of the landmark relationships that kept their faith in the institution alive. I recalled that in the midst of the turmoil of the final days of my marriage, most observers still saw an outwardly happy couple.

I thought about another married couple, one I'd envied as my own marriage was dissolving; he a successful executive, she a prodigious professional as well, both extremely attractive people in their 30s, with a bouncing baby and fashionable Pacific Heights Victorian home.

My former wife and I attended a splendid party there. The couple was perfect; the baby was perfect; the jobs were perfect; the place was perfect; the divorce was perfect. She left him for another man, taking their infant across the country and plunging her husband into a giant economy-sized bottle of Prozac.

I thought about my parents' marriage and their parents' marriage. I began to consider the vast differences between their world and ours. My grandparents didn't own a car, lived their lives not only within a single city but predominantly within a single neighborhood. They were seldom exposed to people of different origins or backgrounds. Rather, they were vacuum packed in the attitudes and values of a minuscule geographic area, where divorce was rarer than the California condor, divorces were accompanied by community-wide incredulity, whispers, or sneers, and the pool of singles past the age of 25 was virtually nonexistent.

By contrast, today most of us think nothing of flying about the country, visiting cultures around the globe, or watching live warfare on the other side of the planet in the comfort of our living rooms. Single people of every age are everywhere, divorce is as ubiquitous as the flu, and the only thing you can really count on is change.

In short, people do, think, read, watch, encounter, even eat, things our grandparents never dreamed of. *Yet we expect their institutions to work for us.* We've inherited their dreams. But we have very different realities.

Our grandparents and parents often held homes for a lifetime. We hold them until we can trade up. We change jobs, cities, cars, and attitudes with a speed that our forebears would hardly believe. Why not relationships? In a rapidly changing, disposable world, is anything immune?

"It's really a throwaway society, isn't it?" said Paul Newman in a Barbara Walters special on the subject of romance. "You throw away everything. You throw away your institutions, your faith in Congress, the Supreme Court, marriage, church . . . Everything is under attack. You throw away bottles, cans . . . We throw away wives, children, careers, whatever. So we [Joanne and he] recycle all the bottles. We try to fix the toaster instead of throwing it away. And when we get in trouble, we try to fix it."

That's easy for him to say. *Our* lives, we complain, are complex and out of hand, and we're neurotic and pressured and going through another crisis, ad nauseam. How can you expect a relationship to work with all that going on?

Simple. You don't *expect* it.

Certainly, all the complexities of your life may be true; may be harrowing, time consuming, anguishing. But they're all beside the point unless you are going to allow the outside circumstances of your life to define you and ultimately determine the destiny of your relationships.

If you genuinely want to make a life of sharing and continuity with another person, you've got to step up to the plate and commit, truly commit, and recommit constantly.

Paste a copy of those marriage vows to the refrigerator, pal. There's nothing else in life that you promise "till death do you part." Remember the agreement: for better or worse, for richer or for poorer, in sickness and in health. "For poorer" means *for poorer.* "In sickness" isn't limited to tennis elbow. *What part of the promise don't you understand?* How many times have you heard people say, "My relationship isn't working." What does this mean, "not working"? Didn't your parents tell you that you have to *make* relationships work? Relationships *don't work,* at least not by themselves, like a car or a Cuisinart.

On the following pages are 100 ways to help work at it, if you're among those fortunate enough to really love and be loved by another soul on this planet. But a *million* ways wouldn't be enough without the understanding that a relationship is a process, not a product.

I'll give you the 101st suggestion; it's not on the list: If you love someone, marry them.

Obviously, marriage is neither a panacea nor a guarantee. But it is a commitment, and like most commitments, the times it's needed most are the bad times, stressful times, when all agreements are put to the test. Couples seldom need much to hold them together when they're sunning on the beach in Ocho Rios. But marriage just might be the thing that gives you that extra fraction of staying power, the extra impetus to work at it just a little harder and a little longer. After all, in the turbulent hours of a relationship, how can you keep a promise that you never made in the first place?

Maybe you should ask yourself whether you're suitable material for a lasting relationship at all. Mae West once said, "Marriage is a great institution. But I'm not ready for an institution."

Are *you* ready for one? Can you give and share and love someone devotedly and unselfishly? Can you expand your identity enough to truly include another person, so that their dreams and doubts and pain and pleasure are virtually indistinguishable from your own? Can you simultaneously be accepting enough to let them be separate and free?

If you answered yes to these questions, you may be eligible to win a trip for two that actually lasts a lifetime: a genuinely fulfilling, evolving, accepting, enduring, loving relationship.

The few who share one will tell you that nothing's more precious. I hear that some are even living happily ever after.

THE 100 BEST WAYS TO STAY TOGETHER

1. Communicate.

2. Communicate.

3. Communicate.

4. No matter what you do at work, be equals at home.

5. Don't hog the remote.

6. If you don't want to talk about it,
it's the first thing you should
talk about.

7. If you get too busy for intimacy, change your priorities.

8. Agree on priorities.

9. Don't bring preconceived ideas of the perfect partner into a relationship; your partner is somebody else.

10. Don't use sex manipulatively.

11. Don't use money manipulatively.

12. Share housework and swap chores. (In a poll that asked women whether they'd rather watch a man dance naked or wash dishes, 61 percent chose dishes!)

13. Dance naked while you wash dishes.

14. Take long walks, bike rides, and drives together with no destination in mind.

15. Look at every misunderstanding as a road to understanding.

16. Get to the bottom of serial arguments.

17. *Date* your partner,
even if you're both 90.

18. Keep time together sacred.

19. Keep time alone sacred.

20. Make love religiously.

21. Recognize that she was raised in a world that discriminated against her in both obvious and subtle ways—and still does.

22. Recognize that he was raised in a world that stereotyped him and subjected him to insidious pressures—and still does.

23. Expect change in the world, yourself, your partner, and your relationship.

24. Remember the past,
plan for the future,
live in the present.

25. Drop everything and go out for a movie and ice cream, or a night at a great B & B, or a weekend at the beach.

26. Respect her career, avocations, and ambitions as much as your own. Do the same for him.

27. Put your relationship above your career, avocations, and ambitions.

28. Make realistic plans.

29. Always have a dream.

30. Surprise her with flowers or a book or concert tickets. (They're no surprise on a birthday or anniversary.)

31. Remember birthdays and anniversaries.

32. Surprise *him* with flowers or a six-pack of microbrew or baseball tickets. (A recent study indicates that couples who go to ball games together are 23 percent less likely to get divorced!)

33. Pay attention to the little things.

34. Don't dwell on the little things.

35. Hug.

36. If it's serious to your partner, *it's serious.*

37. Don't take yourself too seriously.

38. Don't feud with an audience present.

39. Fight fair.

40. Don't fight to win; fight to *tie*.

41. *Make making up so much fun, you almost look forward to a fight.*

42. Be spontaneous.

43. *Learn patience.*

44. Be liberal with compliments.

45. Be gentle with criticisms.

46. Be extravagant with encouragement.

47. Say please and thank-you.

48. Be considerate.

49. Be empathetic.

50. Be giving.

51. *Be on time!*

52. Be clear about how you feel about having children.

53. Don't let having children displace your relationship.

54. Treasure your children.

55. *Never compete for your children's affection.*

56. Don't get into the habit of waiting to make love until everything else is done.

57. Don't confide too much about your relationship to others.

58. Watch for subtle signals in your partner's behavior.

59. Watch for subtle signals in your own behavior.

60. Develop mutual early-warning systems.

61. *Never assume.*

62. Make frequent reality checks.

63. Confront problems before they confront you.

64. Admit it when you're wrong.

65. Be a gracious winner.

66. Coordinate your religious convictions.

67. Support a charity or cause together.

68. Never have sex out of obligation.

69. Respect your partner's separateness.

70. Respect your own separateness.

71. Remember what it was like to be single.

72. If you take your partner for granted, someone else may not.

73. Share fantasies *(and grant them whenever you can).*

74. Don't get sloppy about your appearance.

75. Break patterns.

76. *Be there.*

77. Be honest with your partner.

78. Be honest with yourself.

79. Never have a secret agenda.

80. Don't cheat. Period.

81. Say "I love you" often.
(But not so often that you devalue
its meaning.)

82. If you can't say it, write it.

83. *Call.*

84. Don't make your partner the object of jokes.

85. Talk through your fears.

86. Learn about your partner's parents' relationship; it may explain a lot.

87. Learn everything there is to know about *yourself*.

88. When you're thinking about the negative things, consider they're part of the package. (And remember your own four or five worst traits.)

89. Remember, pure probability says there's a 50-50 chance that you're wrong, and an even greater chance that you're at least half wrong.

90. While you're waiting for your partner's behavior to change, consider how hard it is to change your *own* behavior.

91. Don't assume that you're too smart or that it's too late for counseling.

92. *Be vulnerable.*

93. See the movies *When Harry Met Sally*, *Same Time Next Year,* and *Two for the Road.*

94. Set few rules besides honesty and fidelity.

95. Remember John Lennon's words,
"Life is what happens
while you're making plans."

96. Consider that joy shared is doubled, and that pain shared is halved.

97. *Be each other's best friend.*

98. Touch.

99. Prize laughter.

100. Love life.

AFTERWORD

Okay, you've flipped through *The 100 Best Ways to Stay Together*.

If you liked it and think it might be of value in your relationship, stop here, and enjoy.

If, on the other hand, your relationship is in stress, if you don't want to hug and visit new byways, if you feel your relationship is somehow different than it used to be, or that one or both of you have changed, maybe so. But maybe something has *reverted*.

I have this theory. I call it "time-release behavior." Here's how it goes: You get this subconscious blueprint at one point in time, and you put it in suspended animation until another point in time, when the right circumstance causes it to animate.

I came up with this theory during the dissolution of my own lengthy, and largely happy, marriage. It was then, with the aid of a sensational therapist, that both my ex-wife and I became aware of things set into motion long before we met.

Consider that people are rarely *taught* anything about relationships. We take lessons or courses in everything from tennis to trigonometry, but few of us actively learn about relationships or parenting. We grab a book or two when we're in trouble, but for the most part we're pretty much expected to *know* intuitively about what may be life's most complicated subject.

So where *do* we learn what we learn?

You may not like the idea, but in all likelihood, the source of your education about marriage was long ago, day in and day out, from the vantage point of a growing child—taught by example by dear old Dad and Mom. You weren't conscious of it, you may have even rebelled against it in high school or college. But as surely as you learned about guy things watching your dad, and girl things watching your mom, you also spent years of intimate, thorough, daily observation of one particular marriage, *the* marriage. And all that time, you unknowingly created your own subconscious blueprint of spousal and parental roles. (Remember that this has been borne out in studies of children from abusive families, alcoholic families, and Nobel Prize–winning families.)

In my marriage, it took having a child to trigger the phenomenon. (Don't get me wrong, my son is the best thing that ever happened to me.) But before then, my ex-wife and I pretty much invented our relationship as we went along, and it bore no resemblance to our parents' marriages.

Then, after years of camping in the Sierra, wine tasting in Napa Valley, and antiques shopping in the nooks of San Francisco, our child was born and we up and moved from a carefree condo to a house in the burbs, with a stationwagon and a yard the size of Montana.

Bingo. A house, car, baby, all triggering a long-awaited conditioned response. (Your triggers may vary.)

Then much more than external circumstances began to change. Without much thought, we slowly and imperceptibly slid into roles that mimicked our parents' during our own respective childhoods. I commuted and did the work/achievement thing, like my dad so many years before. She pretty much ceased working and did the Donna Reed thing, just like her mother had.

What's so bad about this picture? Simple, *my* father would have made a miserable match for *her* mother!

My dad was a professional and civic leader who, had he not personally paid the gardener, would have thought roses and violets grew automatically. And as the joke goes, what my mother made for dinner was reservations.

Try mixing and matching those two with my former salt-of-the-earth, workshop-in-the-basement, dirt-under-his-fingernails father-in-law, and his wife who served home-cooked dinners and fresh key lime pie nightly, just as my parents were dressing for the theater.

So almost two decades later, here are my ex-wife and I struggling with our new roles, behaving very differently than ever before. Suddenly she's the consummate homebody and I'm the success-driven overachiever. The transformation was complete; our parents (or some insidious part of them) had inhabited our bodies, and we didn't know it!

"What about the leaves in the rain gutters?" "We can pay someone to do that; let's go to Yosemite!" "Why don't you appreciate my tomato garden?" "Up till now the tomatoes at Safeway have been just fine; why don't you appreciate my promotion?"

If only I'd known why and how important

those tomatoes were to her, maybe I'd have grown salad dressing!

The point is, you can't take behavior at face value—yours or anyone else's. You need frequent reality checks. You have to know who's in the present and what's in the past. Time-release behavior.

Before you scrap a relationship, consider that it may be worth taking a long look *backward* to learn what are the tomatoes in your relationship.

With any luck, instead of breaking up, you could be making pasta.